Booker T. Washington

Published in the United States of America by Cherry Lake Publishing
Ann Arbor, Michigan
www.cherrylakepublishing.com

Content Adviser: Ryan Emery Hughes, Doctoral Student, School of Education, University of Michigan
Reading Adviser: Marla Conn MS, Ed., Literacy specialist, Read-Ability, Inc.
Book Design: Jennifer Wahi
Illustrator: Jeff Bane

Photo Credits: © Carol M. Highsmith/Library of Congress, 5; © The Story of My Life and Work (1901)/archive.org, 7; © The Elementary Spelling Book (1866)/archive.org, 9; © Frances Benjamin Johnston Collection (Library of Congress), 11, 15;© Booker T. Washington Collection (Library of Congress), 13; © Detroit Publishing Co./Library of Congress, 17; © Everett Historical/Shutterstock, 19; © Harris & Ewing/Library of Congress, 21; Cover,8, 10, 18, Jeff Bane; Various frames throughout, Shutterstock Images

Library of Congress Cataloging-in-Publication Data

Names: Haldy, Emma E., author.
Title: Booker T. Washington / Emma E. Haldy.
Description: Ann Arbor : Cherry Lake Publishing, [2016] | Series: My itty-bitty bio | Includes bibliographical references and index. | Audience: Grades K-3.
Identifiers: LCCN 2015045145| ISBN 9781634710183 (hardcover) | ISBN 9781634711173 (pdf) | ISBN 9781634712163 (pbk.) | ISBN 9781634713153 (ebook)
Subjects: LCSH: Washington, Booker T., 1856-1915--Juvenile literature. | African Americans--Biography--Juvenile literature. | Educators--United States--Biography--Juvenile literature.
Classification: LCC E185.97.W4 H35 2016 | DDC 370.92--dc23
LC record available at http://lccn.loc.gov/2015045145
2015026236

Printed in the United States of America
Corporate Graphics

About the author: Emma E. Haldy is a former librarian and a proud Michigander. She lives with her husband, Joe, and an ever-growing collection of books.

About the illustrator: Jeff Bane and his two business partners own a studio along the American River in Folsom, California, home of the 1849 Gold Rush. When Jeff's not sketching or illustrating for clients, he's either swimming or kayaking in the river to relax.

I was born in Virginia. It was 1856.

I was black. I came from a family of **slaves**.

Where and when were you born?

Slavery ended when I was nine. I was free. My family was free.

But we were poor. I had to work.

I wanted to go to school.
My mother understood.
She supported me.

She bought me a book.
I taught myself to read.

I had to keep working.
But I also went to school.

I worked my way through college. I became a teacher.

I was asked to lead a new school. It was in Tuskegee, Alabama.

It was a school for black people. It had few **resources**. I knew I could help.

Why is it important to go to school?

The school taught trades.
Students learned skills.
They joined the working world.

I wanted them to get jobs.
I wanted them to earn a
good living.

I led Tuskegee to great success. It became strong. It had plenty of resources.

I was proud of my students. I believed in the power of education.

I had other ideas. I thought jobs and money were the best way for blacks to **advance**.

I shared my ideas. I wrote books. I formed groups. I gave speeches.

I worked to help my community until my death.

I was a **self-made** man. I was a **champion** of education.

What would you like to ask me?

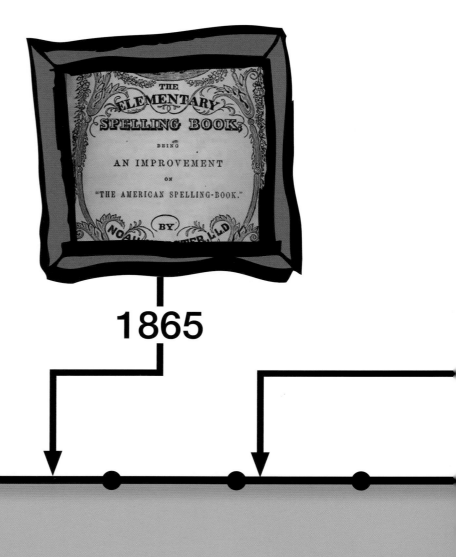

1865

1850

Born
1856

1881

1950

↑
Died
1915

23

glossary

advance (uhd-VANS) to move forward

champion (CHAM-pee-uhn) a person who stands up for another person or an idea

resources (REE-sors-sez) money or other useful things

self-made (self-MAYD) successful because of hard work

slaves (SLAYVZ) people who are owned by other people

index